This Journal Belong to:

_____

_____

Date _____   Source of Anxiety _____

Time _____   Physical Sensations _____

Place _____

Negative Beliefs

About Yourself	About Situation

What facts do you know are true?

About Yourself	About Situation

Color where you feel
sensations of anxiety

Is there a more balanced way to think about this situation

What has helped before?

What is helping now?

Coping Mechanisms

Breathe
Remind yourself that anxiety is just a feeling
Describe your surroundings in detail
Go outdoors
Sip a warm or iced drink slowly
Ground yourself

Date _____   Source of Anxiety _____

Time _____   Physical Sensations _____

Place _____

Negative Beliefs

About Yourself	About Situation

What facts do you know are true?

About Yourself	About Situation

Color where you feel
sensations of anxiety

Is there a more balanced way to think about this situation

What has helped before?   What is helping now?

Coping Mechanisms

Breathe
Remind yourself that anxiety is just a feeling
Describe your surroundings in detail
Go outdoors
Sip a warm or iced drink slowly
Ground yourself

Date _____   Source of Anxiety _____

Time _____   Physical Sensations _____

Place _____

Negative Beliefs

About Yourself	About Situation

What facts do you know are true?

About Yourself	About Situation

Color where you feel
sensations of anxiety

Is there a more balanced way to think about this situation

What has helped before?   What is helping now?

Coping Mechanisms

Breathe
Remind yourself that anxiety is just a feeling
Describe your surroundings in detail
Go outdoors
Sip a warm or iced drink slowly
Ground yourself

Date _____ Source of Anxiety _____

Time _____ Physical Sensations _____

Place _____

Negative Beliefs

About Yourself	About Situation

What facts do you know are true?

About Yourself	About Situation

Color where you feel
sensations of anxiety

Is there a more balanced way to think about this situation

What has helped before?

What is helping now?

Coping Mechanisms

Breathe
Remind yourself that anxiety is just a feeling
Describe your surroundings in detail
Go outdoors
Sip a warm or iced drink slowly
Ground yourself

Date _____   Source of Anxiety _____

Time _____   Physical Sensations _____

Place _____

Negative Beliefs

About Yourself	About Situation

What facts do you know are true?

About Yourself	About Situation

Color where you feel
sensations of anxiety

Is there a more balanced way to think about this situation

What has helped before?

What is helping now?

Coping Mechanisms

Breathe
Remind yourself that anxiety is just a feeling
Describe your surroundings in detail
Go outdoors
Sip a warm or iced drink slowly
Ground yourself

Date _____   Source of Anxiety _____

Time _____   Physical Sensations _____

Place _____

Negative Beliefs

About Yourself	About Situation

What facts do you know are true?

About Yourself	About Situation

Color where you feel
sensations of anxiety

Is there a more balanced way to think about this situation

What has helped before?

What is helping now?

Coping Mechanisms

Breathe
Remind yourself that anxiety is just a feeling
Describe your surroundings in detail
Go outdoors
Sip a warm or iced drink slowly
Ground yourself

Date _____   Source of Anxiety _____

Time _____   Physical Sensations _____

Place _____

Negative Beliefs

About Yourself	About Situation

What facts do you know are true?

About Yourself	About Situation

Color where you feel
sensations of anxiety

Is there a more balanced way to think about this situation

What has helped before?   What is helping now?

—————— Coping Mechanisms ——————

Breathe
Remind yourself that anxiety is just a feeling
Describe your surroundings in detail
Go outdoors
Sip a warm or iced drink slowly
Ground yourself

Date _____   Source of Anxiety _____

Time _____   Physical Sensations _____

Place _____

Negative Beliefs

About Yourself	About Situation

What facts do you know are true?

About Yourself	About Situation

Color where you feel
sensations of anxiety

Is there a more balanced way to think about this situation

What has helped before?   ## What is helping now?

-------- Coping Mechanisms --------

Breathe
Remind yourself that anxiety is just a feeling
Describe your surroundings in detail
Go outdoors
Sip a warm or iced drink slowly
Ground yourself

Date _____   Source of Anxiety _____

Time _____   Physical Sensations _____

Place _____

Negative Beliefs

About Yourself	About Situation

What facts do you know are true?

About Yourself	About Situation

Color where you feel
sensations of anxiety

Is there a more balanced way to think about this situation

What has helped before?   What is helping now?

—————————————— Coping Mechanisms ——————————————

Breathe
Remind yourself that anxiety is just a feeling
Describe your surroundings in detail
Go outdoors
Sip a warm or iced drink slowly
Ground yourself

Date _____   Source of Anxiety _____

Time _____   Physical Sensations _____

Place _____

Negative Beliefs

About Yourself	About Situation

What facts do you know are true?

About Yourself	About Situation

Color where you feel
sensations of anxiety

Is there a more balanced way to think about this situation

What has helped before?   What is helping now?

Coping Mechanisms

Breathe
Remind yourself that anxiety is just a feeling
Describe your surroundings in detail
Go outdoors
Sip a warm or iced drink slowly
Ground yourself

Date _____   Source of Anxiety _____

Time _____   Physical Sensations _____

Place _____

Negative Beliefs

About Yourself	About Situation

What facts do you know are true?

About Yourself	About Situation

Color where you feel
sensations of anxiety

Is there a more balanced way to think about this situation

What has helped before?   ## What is helping now?

Coping Mechanisms

Breathe
Remind yourself that anxiety is just a feeling
Describe your surroundings in detail
Go outdoors
Sip a warm or iced drink slowly
Ground yourself

Date _____   Source of Anxiety _____

Time _____   Physical Sensations _____
                                              _____
Place _____

Negative Beliefs

About Yourself	About Situation

What facts do you know are true?

About Yourself	About Situation

Color where you feel
sensations of anxiety

Is there a more balanced way to think about this situation

What has helped before?   What is helping now?

──────────── Coping Mechanisms ────────────

Breathe
Remind yourself that anxiety is just a feeling
Describe your surroundings in detail
Go outdoors
Sip a warm or iced drink slowly
Ground yourself

Date _____   Source of Anxiety _____

Time _____   Physical Sensations _____

Place _____

Negative Beliefs

About Yourself	About Situation

What facts do you know are true?

About Yourself	About Situation

Color where you feel
sensations of anxiety

Is there a more balanced way to think about this situation

What has helped before?

What is helping now?

Coping Mechanisms

Breathe
Remind yourself that anxiety is just a feeling
Describe your surroundings in detail
Go outdoors
Sip a warm or iced drink slowly
Ground yourself

Date _____   Source of Anxiety _____

Time _____   Physical Sensations _____

Place _____

Negative Beliefs

About Yourself	About Situation

What facts do you know are true?

About Yourself	About Situation

Color where you feel
sensations of anxiety

Is there a more balanced way to think about this situation

What has helped before?

What is helping now?

Coping Mechanisms

Breathe
Remind yourself that anxiety is just a feeling
Describe your surroundings in detail
Go outdoors
Sip a warm or iced drink slowly
Ground yourself

Date _____   Source of Anxiety _____

Time _____   Physical Sensations _____

Place _____

Negative Beliefs

About Yourself	About Situation

What facts do you know are true?

About Yourself	About Situation

Color where you feel
sensations of anxiety

Is there a more balanced way to think about this situation

What has helped before?

What is helping now?

Coping Mechanisms

Breathe
Remind yourself that anxiety is just a feeling
Describe your surroundings in detail
Go outdoors
Sip a warm or iced drink slowly
Ground yourself

Date _____   Source of Anxiety _____

Time _____   Physical Sensations _____

Place _____

Negative Beliefs

About Yourself	About Situation

What facts do you know are true?

About Yourself	About Situation

Color where you feel
sensations of anxiety

Is there a more balanced way to think about this situation

What has helped before?   What is helping now?

Coping Mechanisms

Breathe
Remind yourself that anxiety is just a feeling
Describe your surroundings in detail
Go outdoors
Sip a warm or iced drink slowly
Ground yourself

Date _____   Source of Anxiety _____

Time _____   Physical Sensations _____

Place _____

Negative Beliefs

About Yourself	About Situation

What facts do you know are true?

About Yourself	About Situation

Color where you feel
sensations of anxiety

Is there a more balanced way to think about this situation

What has helped before?   What is helping now?

Coping Mechanisms

Breathe
Remind yourself that anxiety is just a feeling
Describe your surroundings in detail
Go outdoors
Sip a warm or iced drink slowly
Ground yourself

Date _____   Source of Anxiety _____

Time _____   Physical Sensations _____

Place _____

Negative Beliefs

About Yourself	About Situation

What facts do you know are true?

About Yourself	About Situation

Color where you feel
sensations of anxiety

Is there a more balanced way to think about this situation

What has helped before?   ## What is helping now?

Coping Mechanisms

Breathe
Remind yourself that anxiety is just a feeling
Describe your surroundings in detail
Go outdoors
Sip a warm or iced drink slowly
Ground yourself

Date _____   Source of Anxiety _____

Time _____   Physical Sensations _____

Place _____

Negative Beliefs

About Yourself	About Situation

What facts do you know are true?

About Yourself	About Situation

Color where you feel
sensations of anxiety

Is there a more balanced way to think about this situation

What has helped before?   What is helping now?

Coping Mechanisms

Breathe
Remind yourself that anxiety is just a feeling
Describe your surroundings in detail
Go outdoors
Sip a warm or iced drink slowly
Ground yourself

Date _____   Source of Anxiety _____

Time _____   Physical Sensations _____

Place _____

Negative Beliefs

About Yourself	About Situation

What facts do you know are true?

About Yourself	About Situation

Color where you feel
sensations of anxiety

Is there a more balanced way to think about this situation

What has helped before?   What is helping now?

Coping Mechanisms

Breathe
Remind yourself that anxiety is just a feeling
Describe your surroundings in detail
Go outdoors
Sip a warm or iced drink slowly
Ground yourself

Date _____   Source of Anxiety _____

Time _____   Physical Sensations _____

Place _____

Negative Beliefs

About Yourself	About Situation

What facts do you know are true?

About Yourself	About Situation

Color where you feel
sensations of anxiety

Is there a more balanced way to think about this situation

What has helped before?

What is helping now?

Coping Mechanisms

Breathe
Remind yourself that anxiety is just a feeling
Describe your surroundings in detail
Go outdoors
Sip a warm or iced drink slowly
Ground yourself

Date _____   Source of Anxiety _____

Time _____   Physical Sensations _____

Place _____

Negative Beliefs

About Yourself	About Situation

What facts do you know are true?

About Yourself	About Situation

Color where you feel
sensations of anxiety

Is there a more balanced way to think about this situation

What has helped before?   What is helping now?

Coping Mechanisms

Breathe
Remind yourself that anxiety is just a feeling
Describe your surroundings in detail
Go outdoors
Sip a warm or iced drink slowly
Ground yourself

Date _____   Source of Anxiety _____

Time _____   Physical Sensations _____

Place _____

Negative Beliefs

About Yourself	About Situation

What facts do you know are true?

About Yourself	About Situation

Color where you feel
sensations of anxiety

Is there a more balanced way to think about this situation

What has helped before?

What is helping now?

Coping Mechanisms

Breathe
Remind yourself that anxiety is just a feeling
Describe your surroundings in detail
Go outdoors
Sip a warm or iced drink slowly
Ground yourself

Date _____   Source of Anxiety _____

Time _____   Physical Sensations _____

Place _____

Negative Beliefs

About Yourself	About Situation

What facts do you know are true?

About Yourself	About Situation

Color where you feel
sensations of anxiety

Is there a more balanced way to think about this situation

What has helped before?   What is helping now?

──────────── Coping Mechanisms ────────────

Breathe
Remind yourself that anxiety is just a feeling
Describe your surroundings in detail
Go outdoors
Sip a warm or iced drink slowly
Ground yourself

Date _____   Source of Anxiety _____

Time _____   Physical Sensations _____

Place _____

Negative Beliefs

About Yourself	About Situation

What facts do you know are true?

About Yourself	About Situation

Color where you feel
sensations of anxiety

Is there a more balanced way to think about this situation

What has helped before?

What is helping now?

─── Coping Mechanisms ───

Breathe
Remind yourself that anxiety is just a feeling
Describe your surroundings in detail
Go outdoors
Sip a warm or iced drink slowly
Ground yourself

Date _____   Source of Anxiety _____

Time _____   Physical Sensations _____

Place _____

Negative Beliefs

About Yourself	About Situation

What facts do you know are true?

About Yourself	About Situation

Color where you feel
sensations of anxiety

Is there a more balanced way to think about this situation

What has helped before?

What is helping now?

Coping Mechanisms

Breathe
Remind yourself that anxiety is just a feeling
Describe your surroundings in detail
Go outdoors
Sip a warm or iced drink slowly
Ground yourself

Date _____   Source of Anxiety _____

Time _____   Physical Sensations _____

Place _____

Negative Beliefs

About Yourself	About Situation

What facts do you know are true?

About Yourself	About Situation

Color where you feel
sensations of anxiety

Is there a more balanced way to think about this situation

What has helped before?

What is helping now?

Coping Mechanisms

Breathe
Remind yourself that anxiety is just a feeling
Describe your surroundings in detail
Go outdoors
Sip a warm or iced drink slowly
Ground yourself

Date _____   Source of Anxiety _____

Time _____   Physical Sensations _____

Place _____

Negative Beliefs

About Yourself	About Situation

What facts do you know are true?

About Yourself	About Situation

Color where you feel
sensations of anxiety

Is there a more balanced way to think about this situation

What has helped before?   What is helping now?

——— Coping Mechanisms ———

Breathe
Remind yourself that anxiety is just a feeling
Describe your surroundings in detail
Go outdoors
Sip a warm or iced drink slowly
Ground yourself

Date _____   Source of Anxiety _____

Time _____   Physical Sensations _____

Place _____

Negative Beliefs

About Yourself	About Situation

What facts do you know are true?

About Yourself	About Situation

Color where you feel
sensations of anxiety

Is there a more balanced way to think about this situation

What has helped before?   What is helping now?

────────── Coping Mechanisms ──────────

Breathe
Remind yourself that anxiety is just a feeling
Describe your surroundings in detail
Go outdoors
Sip a warm or iced drink slowly
Ground yourself

Date _____   Source of Anxiety _____

Time _____   Physical Sensations _____

Place _____

Negative Beliefs

About Yourself	About Situation

What facts do you know are true?

About Yourself	About Situation

Color where you feel
sensations of anxiety

Is there a more balanced way to think about this situation

What has helped before?   What is helping now?

Coping Mechanisms

Breathe
Remind yourself that anxiety is just a feeling
Describe your surroundings in detail
Go outdoors
Sip a warm or iced drink slowly
Ground yourself

Date _____   Source of Anxiety _____

Time _____   Physical Sensations _____

Place _____

Negative Beliefs

About Yourself	About Situation

What facts do you know are true?

About Yourself	About Situation

Color where you feel
sensations of anxiety

Is there a more balanced way to think about this situation

What has helped before?

What is helping now?

──── Coping Mechanisms ────

Breathe
Remind yourself that anxiety is just a feeling
Describe your surroundings in detail
Go outdoors
Sip a warm or iced drink slowly
Ground yourself

Date _____   Source of Anxiety _____

Time _____   Physical Sensations _____

Place _____

Negative Beliefs

About Yourself	About Situation

What facts do you know are true?

About Yourself	About Situation

Color where you feel
sensations of anxiety

Is there a more balanced way to think about this situation

What has helped before?   What is helping now?

——— Coping Mechanisms ———

Breathe
Remind yourself that anxiety is just a feeling
Describe your surroundings in detail
Go outdoors
Sip a warm or iced drink slowly
Ground yourself

Date _____   Source of Anxiety _____

Time _____   Physical Sensations _____

Place _____

Negative Beliefs

About Yourself	About Situation

What facts do you know are true?

About Yourself	About Situation

Color where you feel
sensations of anxiety

Is there a more balanced way to think about this situation

What has helped before?   ## What is helping now?

——————— Coping Mechanisms ———————

Breathe
Remind yourself that anxiety is just a feeling
Describe your surroundings in detail
Go outdoors
Sip a warm or iced drink slowly
Ground yourself

Date _____   Source of Anxiety _____

Time _____   Physical Sensations _____

Place _____

Negative Beliefs

About Yourself	About Situation

What facts do you know are true?

About Yourself	About Situation

Color where you feel
sensations of anxiety

Is there a more balanced way to think about this situation

What has helped before?   ## What is helping now?

Coping Mechanisms

Breathe
Remind yourself that anxiety is just a feeling
Describe your surroundings in detail
Go outdoors
Sip a warm or iced drink slowly
Ground yourself

Date _____   Source of Anxiety _____

Time _____   Physical Sensations _____

Place _____

Negative Beliefs

About Yourself	About Situation

What facts do you know are true?

About Yourself	About Situation

Color where you feel
sensations of anxiety

Is there a more balanced way to think about this situation

What has helped before?   ## What is helping now?

─── Coping Mechanisms ───

Breathe
Remind yourself that anxiety is just a feeling
Describe your surroundings in detail
Go outdoors
Sip a warm or iced drink slowly
Ground yourself

Date _____   Source of Anxiety _____

Time _____   Physical Sensations _____

Place _____

Negative Beliefs

About Yourself	About Situation

What facts do you know are true?

About Yourself	About Situation

Color where you feel
sensations of anxiety

Is there a more balanced way to think about this situation

What has helped before?

What is helping now?

Coping Mechanisms

Breathe
Remind yourself that anxiety is just a feeling
Describe your surroundings in detail
Go outdoors
Sip a warm or iced drink slowly
Ground yourself

Date _____   Source of Anxiety _____

Time _____   Physical Sensations _____

Place _____

Negative Beliefs

About Yourself	About Situation

What facts do you know are true?

About Yourself	About Situation

Color where you feel
sensations of anxiety

Is there a more balanced way to think about this situation

What has helped before?   What is helping now?

--- Coping Mechanisms ---

Breathe
Remind yourself that anxiety is just a feeling
Describe your surroundings in detail
Go outdoors
Sip a warm or iced drink slowly
Ground yourself

Date _____   Source of Anxiety _____

Time _____   Physical Sensations _____

Place _____

Negative Beliefs

About Yourself	About Situation

What facts do you know are true?

About Yourself	About Situation

Color where you feel
sensations of anxiety

Is there a more balanced way to think about this situation

What has helped before?

What is helping now?

Coping Mechanisms

Breathe
Remind yourself that anxiety is just a feeling
Describe your surroundings in detail
Go outdoors
Sip a warm or iced drink slowly
Ground yourself

Date _____   Source of Anxiety _____

Time _____   Physical Sensations _____

Place _____

Negative Beliefs

About Yourself	About Situation

What facts do you know are true?

About Yourself	About Situation

Color where you feel
sensations of anxiety

Is there a more balanced way to think about this situation

What has helped before?   What is helping now?

──── Coping Mechanisms ────

Breathe
Remind yourself that anxiety is just a feeling
Describe your surroundings in detail
Go outdoors
Sip a warm or iced drink slowly
Ground yourself

Date _____   Source of Anxiety _____

Time _____   Physical Sensations _____

Place _____

Negative Beliefs

About Yourself	About Situation

What facts do you know are true?

About Yourself	About Situation

Color where you feel
sensations of anxiety

Is there a more balanced way to think about this situation

What has helped before?   What is helping now?

Coping Mechanisms

Breathe
Remind yourself that anxiety is just a feeling
Describe your surroundings in detail
Go outdoors
Sip a warm or iced drink slowly
Ground yourself

Date _____   Source of Anxiety _____

Time _____   Physical Sensations _____

Place _____

Negative Beliefs

About Yourself	About Situation

What facts do you know are true?

About Yourself	About Situation

Color where you feel
sensations of anxiety

Is there a more balanced way to think about this situation

What has helped before?   What is helping now?

Coping Mechanisms

Breathe
Remind yourself that anxiety is just a feeling
Describe your surroundings in detail
Go outdoors
Sip a warm or iced drink slowly
Ground yourself

Date _____   Source of Anxiety _____

Time _____   Physical Sensations _____

Place _____

Negative Beliefs

About Yourself	About Situation

What facts do you know are true?

About Yourself	About Situation

Color where you feel
sensations of anxiety

Is there a more balanced way to think about this situation

What has helped before?   What is helping now?

Coping Mechanisms

Breathe
Remind yourself that anxiety is just a feeling
Describe your surroundings in detail
Go outdoors
Sip a warm or iced drink slowly
Ground yourself

Date _____   Source of Anxiety _____

Time _____   Physical Sensations _____

Place _____

Negative Beliefs

About Yourself	About Situation

What facts do you know are true?

About Yourself	About Situation

Color where you feel
sensations of anxiety

Is there a more balanced way to think about this situation

What has helped before?   What is helping now?

Coping Mechanisms

Breathe
Remind yourself that anxiety is just a feeling
Describe your surroundings in detail
Go outdoors
Sip a warm or iced drink slowly
Ground yourself

Date _____   Source of Anxiety _____

Time _____   Physical Sensations _____

Place _____

Negative Beliefs

About Yourself	About Situation

What facts do you know are true?

About Yourself	About Situation

Color where you feel
sensations of anxiety

Is there a more balanced way to think about this situation

What has helped before?   What is helping now?

Coping Mechanisms

Breathe
Remind yourself that anxiety is just a feeling
Describe your surroundings in detail
Go outdoors
Sip a warm or iced drink slowly
Ground yourself

Date _____   Source of Anxiety _____

Time _____   Physical Sensations _____

Place _____

Negative Beliefs

About Yourself	About Situation

What facts do you know are true?

About Yourself	About Situation

Color where you feel
sensations of anxiety

Is there a more balanced way to think about this situation

What has helped before?

What is helping now?

Coping Mechanisms

Breathe
Remind yourself that anxiety is just a feeling
Describe your surroundings in detail
Go outdoors
Sip a warm or iced drink slowly
Ground yourself

Date _____   Source of Anxiety _____

Time _____   Physical Sensations _____

Place _____

Negative Beliefs

About Yourself	About Situation

What facts do you know are true?

About Yourself	About Situation

Color where you feel
sensations of anxiety

Is there a more balanced way to think about this situation

What has helped before?

What is helping now?

Coping Mechanisms

Breathe
Remind yourself that anxiety is just a feeling
Describe your surroundings in detail
Go outdoors
Sip a warm or iced drink slowly
Ground yourself

Date _____   Source of Anxiety _____

Time _____   Physical Sensations _____

Place _____

Negative Beliefs

About Yourself	About Situation

What facts do you know are true?

About Yourself	About Situation

Color where you feel
sensations of anxiety

Is there a more balanced way to think about this situation

What has helped before?

What is helping now?

Coping Mechanisms

Breathe
Remind yourself that anxiety is just a feeling
Describe your surroundings in detail
Go outdoors
Sip a warm or iced drink slowly
Ground yourself

Date _____   Source of Anxiety _____

Time _____   Physical Sensations _____

Place _____

Negative Beliefs

About Yourself	About Situation

What facts do you know are true?

About Yourself	About Situation

Color where you feel
sensations of anxiety

Is there a more balanced way to think about this situation

What has helped before?   ## What is helping now?

Coping Mechanisms

Breathe
Remind yourself that anxiety is just a feeling
Describe your surroundings in detail
Go outdoors
Sip a warm or iced drink slowly
Ground yourself

Date _____   Source of Anxiety _____

Time _____   Physical Sensations _____

Place _____

Negative Beliefs

About Yourself	About Situation

What facts do you know are true?

About Yourself	About Situation

Color where you feel
sensations of anxiety

Is there a more balanced way to think about this situation

What has helped before?   What is helping now?

──────── Coping Mechanisms ────────

Breathe
Remind yourself that anxiety is just a feeling
Describe your surroundings in detail
Go outdoors
Sip a warm or iced drink slowly
Ground yourself

Date _____   Source of Anxiety _____

Time _____   Physical Sensations _____

Place _____

Negative Beliefs

About Yourself	About Situation

What facts do you know are true?

About Yourself	About Situation

Color where you feel
sensations of anxiety

Is there a more balanced way to think about this situation

What has helped before?   What is helping now?

Coping Mechanisms

Breathe
Remind yourself that anxiety is just a feeling
Describe your surroundings in detail
Go outdoors
Sip a warm or iced drink slowly
Ground yourself

Date _____   Source of Anxiety _____

Time _____   Physical Sensations _____

Place _____

Negative Beliefs

About Yourself	About Situation

What facts do you know are true?

About Yourself	About Situation

Color where you feel
sensations of anxiety

Is there a more balanced way to think about this situation

What has helped before?   What is helping now?

Coping Mechanisms

Breathe
Remind yourself that anxiety is just a feeling
Describe your surroundings in detail
Go outdoors
Sip a warm or iced drink slowly
Ground yourself

Date _____   Source of Anxiety _____

Time _____   Physical Sensations _____

Place _____

Negative Beliefs

About Yourself	About Situation

What facts do you know are true?

About Yourself	About Situation

Color where you feel
sensations of anxiety

Is there a more balanced way to think about this situation

What has helped before?   What is helping now?

─────────── Coping Mechanisms ───────────

Breathe
Remind yourself that anxiety is just a feeling
Describe your surroundings in detail
Go outdoors
Sip a warm or iced drink slowly
Ground yourself

Date _____   Source of Anxiety _____

Time _____   Physical Sensations _____

Place _____

Negative Beliefs

About Yourself	About Situation

What facts do you know are true?

About Yourself	About Situation

Color where you feel
sensations of anxiety

Is there a more balanced way to think about this situation

What has helped before?   What is helping now?

——— Coping Mechanisms ———

Breathe
Remind yourself that anxiety is just a feeling
Describe your surroundings in detail
Go outdoors
Sip a warm or iced drink slowly
Ground yourself

Date _____   Source of Anxiety _____

Time _____   Physical Sensations _____

Place _____

Negative Beliefs

About Yourself	About Situation

What facts do you know are true?

About Yourself	About Situation

Color where you feel
sensations of anxiety

Is there a more balanced way to think about this situation

What has helped before?   What is helping now?

——— Coping Mechanisms ———

Breathe
Remind yourself that anxiety is just a feeling
Describe your surroundings in detail
Go outdoors
Sip a warm or iced drink slowly
Ground yourself

Date _____   Source of Anxiety _____

Time _____   Physical Sensations _____

Place _____

Negative Beliefs

About Yourself	About Situation

What facts do you know are true?

About Yourself	About Situation

Color where you feel
sensations of anxiety

Is there a more balanced way to think about this situation

What has helped before?   What is helping now?

─────────── Coping Mechanisms ───────────

Breathe
Remind yourself that anxiety is just a feeling
Describe your surroundings in detail
Go outdoors
Sip a warm or iced drink slowly
Ground yourself

Date _____   Source of Anxiety _____

Time _____   Physical Sensations _____

Place _____

Negative Beliefs

About Yourself	About Situation

What facts do you know are true?

About Yourself	About Situation

Color where you feel
sensations of anxiety

Is there a more balanced way to think about this situation

What has helped before?

What is helping now?

Coping Mechanisms

Breathe
Remind yourself that anxiety is just a feeling
Describe your surroundings in detail
Go outdoors
Sip a warm or iced drink slowly
Ground yourself

Date _____   Source of Anxiety _____

Time _____   Physical Sensations _____

Place _____

Negative Beliefs

About Yourself	About Situation

What facts do you know are true?

About Yourself	About Situation

Color where you feel
sensations of anxiety

Is there a more balanced way to think about this situation

What has helped before?   What is helping now?

─────────────── Coping Mechanisms ───────────────

Breathe
Remind yourself that anxiety is just a feeling
Describe your surroundings in detail
Go outdoors
Sip a warm or iced drink slowly
Ground yourself

Date _____   Source of Anxiety _____

Time _____   Physical Sensations _____

Place _____

Negative Beliefs

About Yourself	About Situation

What facts do you know are true?

About Yourself	About Situation

Color where you feel
sensations of anxiety

Is there a more balanced way to think about this situation

What has helped before?   What is helping now?

Coping Mechanisms

Breathe
Remind yourself that anxiety is just a feeling
Describe your surroundings in detail
Go outdoors
Sip a warm or iced drink slowly
Ground yourself

Date _____   Source of Anxiety _____

Time _____   Physical Sensations _____

Place _____

Negative Beliefs

About Yourself	About Situation

What facts do you know are true?

About Yourself	About Situation

Color where you feel
sensations of anxiety

Is there a more balanced way to think about this situation

What has helped before?   What is helping now?

──────── Coping Mechanisms ────────

Breathe
Remind yourself that anxiety is just a feeling
Describe your surroundings in detail
Go outdoors
Sip a warm or iced drink slowly
Ground yourself

Date _____   Source of Anxiety _____

Time _____   Physical Sensations _____

Place _____

Negative Beliefs

About Yourself	About Situation

What facts do you know are true?

About Yourself	About Situation

Color where you feel
sensations of anxiety

Is there a more balanced way to think about this situation

What has helped before?   What is helping now?

Coping Mechanisms

Breathe
Remind yourself that anxiety is just a feeling
Describe your surroundings in detail
Go outdoors
Sip a warm or iced drink slowly
Ground yourself

Date _____   Source of Anxiety _____

Time _____   Physical Sensations _____

Place _____

Negative Beliefs

About Yourself	About Situation

What facts do you know are true?

About Yourself	About Situation

Color where you feel
sensations of anxiety

Is there a more balanced way to think about this situation

What has helped before?   What is helping now?

Coping Mechanisms

Breathe
Remind yourself that anxiety is just a feeling
Describe your surroundings in detail
Go outdoors
Sip a warm or iced drink slowly
Ground yourself

Date _____   Source of Anxiety _____

Time _____   Physical Sensations _____

Place _____

Negative Beliefs

About Yourself	About Situation

What facts do you know are true?

About Yourself	About Situation

Color where you feel
sensations of anxiety

Is there a more balanced way to think about this situation

What has helped before?   ## What is helping now?

Coping Mechanisms

Breathe
Remind yourself that anxiety is just a feeling
Describe your surroundings in detail
Go outdoors
Sip a warm or iced drink slowly
Ground yourself

Date _____   Source of Anxiety _____

Time _____   Physical Sensations _____

Place _____

Negative Beliefs

About Yourself	About Situation

What facts do you know are true?

About Yourself	About Situation

Color where you feel
sensations of anxiety

Is there a more balanced way to think about this situation

What has helped before?   What is helping now?

Coping Mechanisms

Breathe
Remind yourself that anxiety is just a feeling
Describe your surroundings in detail
Go outdoors
Sip a warm or iced drink slowly
Ground yourself

Date _____   Source of Anxiety _____

Time _____   Physical Sensations _____

Place _____

Negative Beliefs

About Yourself	About Situation

What facts do you know are true?

About Yourself	About Situation

Color where you feel
sensations of anxiety

Is there a more balanced way to think about this situation

What has helped before?   What is helping now?

Coping Mechanisms

Breathe
Remind yourself that anxiety is just a feeling
Describe your surroundings in detail
Go outdoors
Sip a warm or iced drink slowly
Ground yourself

Date _____   Source of Anxiety _____

Time _____   Physical Sensations _____

Place _____

Negative Beliefs

About Yourself	About Situation

What facts do you know are true?

About Yourself	About Situation

Color where you feel
sensations of anxiety

Is there a more balanced way to think about this situation

What has helped before?   ## What is helping now?

Coping Mechanisms

Breathe
Remind yourself that anxiety is just a feeling
Describe your surroundings in detail
Go outdoors
Sip a warm or iced drink slowly
Ground yourself

Date _____   Source of Anxiety _____

Time _____   Physical Sensations _____

Place _____

Negative Beliefs

About Yourself	About Situation

What facts do you know are true?

About Yourself	About Situation

Color where you feel
sensations of anxiety

Is there a more balanced way to think about this situation

What has helped before?   What is helping now?

Coping Mechanisms

Breathe
Remind yourself that anxiety is just a feeling
Describe your surroundings in detail
Go outdoors
Sip a warm or iced drink slowly
Ground yourself

Date _____ Source of Anxiety _____

Time _____ Physical Sensations _____

Place _____

Negative Beliefs

About Yourself	About Situation

What facts do you know are true?

About Yourself	About Situation

Color where you feel
sensations of anxiety

Is there a more balanced way to think about this situation

What has helped before?

What is helping now?

Coping Mechanisms

Breathe
Remind yourself that anxiety is just a feeling
Describe your surroundings in detail
Go outdoors
Sip a warm or iced drink slowly
Ground yourself

Date _____   Source of Anxiety _____

Time _____   Physical Sensations _____

Place _____

Negative Beliefs

About Yourself	About Situation

What facts do you know are true?

About Yourself	About Situation

Color where you feel
sensations of anxiety

Is there a more balanced way to think about this situation

What has helped before?

What is helping now?

Coping Mechanisms

Breathe
Remind yourself that anxiety is just a feeling
Describe your surroundings in detail
Go outdoors
Sip a warm or iced drink slowly
Ground yourself

Date _____   Source of Anxiety _____

Time _____   Physical Sensations _____

Place _____

Negative Beliefs

About Yourself	About Situation

What facts do you know are true?

About Yourself	About Situation

Color where you feel
sensations of anxiety

Is there a more balanced way to think about this situation

What has helped before?   What is helping now?

Coping Mechanisms

Breathe
Remind yourself that anxiety is just a feeling
Describe your surroundings in detail
Go outdoors
Sip a warm or iced drink slowly
Ground yourself

Date _____   Source of Anxiety _____

Time _____   Physical Sensations _____

Place _____

Negative Beliefs

About Yourself	About Situation

What facts do you know are true?

About Yourself	About Situation

Color where you feel
sensations of anxiety

Is there a more balanced way to think about this situation

What has helped before?   What is helping now?

──────── Coping Mechanisms ────────

Breathe
Remind yourself that anxiety is just a feeling
Describe your surroundings in detail
Go outdoors
Sip a warm or iced drink slowly
Ground yourself

Date _____   Source of Anxiety _____

Time _____   Physical Sensations _____

Place _____

Negative Beliefs

About Yourself	About Situation

What facts do you know are true?

About Yourself	About Situation

Color where you feel
sensations of anxiety

Is there a more balanced way to think about this situation

What has helped before?   What is helping now?

―――――――――――― Coping Mechanisms ――――――――――――

Breathe
Remind yourself that anxiety is just a feeling
Describe your surroundings in detail
Go outdoors
Sip a warm or iced drink slowly
Ground yourself

Date _____

Time _____

Place _____

Source of Anxiety _____

Physical Sensations _____

Negative Beliefs

About Yourself	About Situation

What facts do you know are true?

About Yourself	About Situation

Color where you feel
sensations of anxiety

Is there a more balanced way to think about this situation

What has helped before?

What is helping now?

Coping Mechanisms

Breathe
Remind yourself that anxiety is just a feeling
Describe your surroundings in detail
Go outdoors
Sip a warm or iced drink slowly
Ground yourself

Date _____   Source of Anxiety _____

Time _____   Physical Sensations _____

Place _____

Negative Beliefs

About Yourself	About Situation

What facts do you know are true?

About Yourself	About Situation

Color where you feel
sensations of anxiety

Is there a more balanced way to think about this situation

What has helped before?

What is helping now?

Coping Mechanisms

Breathe
Remind yourself that anxiety is just a feeling
Describe your surroundings in detail
Go outdoors
Sip a warm or iced drink slowly
Ground yourself

Date _____   Source of Anxiety _____

Time _____   Physical Sensations _____

Place _____

Negative Beliefs

About Yourself	About Situation

What facts do you know are true?

About Yourself	About Situation

Color where you feel
sensations of anxiety

Is there a more balanced way to think about this situation

What has helped before?   What is helping now?

Coping Mechanisms

Breathe
Remind yourself that anxiety is just a feeling
Describe your surroundings in detail
Go outdoors
Sip a warm or iced drink slowly
Ground yourself

Date _____ Source of Anxiety _____

Time _____ Physical Sensations _____

Place _____

Negative Beliefs

About Yourself	About Situation

What facts do you know are true?

About Yourself	About Situation

Color where you feel
sensations of anxiety

Is there a more balanced way to think about this situation

What has helped before?

What is helping now?

Coping Mechanisms

Breathe
Remind yourself that anxiety is just a feeling
Describe your surroundings in detail
Go outdoors
Sip a warm or iced drink slowly
Ground yourself

Date _____   Source of Anxiety _____

Time _____   Physical Sensations _____

Place _____

Negative Beliefs

About Yourself	About Situation

What facts do you know are true?

About Yourself	About Situation

Color where you feel
sensations of anxiety

Is there a more balanced way to think about this situation

What has helped before?   What is helping now?

───────────── Coping Mechanisms ─────────────

Breathe
Remind yourself that anxiety is just a feeling
Describe your surroundings in detail
Go outdoors
Sip a warm or iced drink slowly
Ground yourself

Date _____   Source of Anxiety _____

Time _____   Physical Sensations _____

Place _____

Negative Beliefs

About Yourself	About Situation

What facts do you know are true?

About Yourself	About Situation

Color where you feel
sensations of anxiety

Is there a more balanced way to think about this situation

What has helped before?   What is helping now?

Coping Mechanisms

Breathe
Remind yourself that anxiety is just a feeling
Describe your surroundings in detail
Go outdoors
Sip a warm or iced drink slowly
Ground yourself

Date _____   Source of Anxiety _____

Time _____   Physical Sensations _____

Place _____

Negative Beliefs

About Yourself	About Situation

What facts do you know are true?

About Yourself	About Situation

Color where you feel
sensations of anxiety

Is there a more balanced way to think about this situation

What has helped before?

What is helping now?

Coping Mechanisms

Breathe
Remind yourself that anxiety is just a feeling
Describe your surroundings in detail
Go outdoors
Sip a warm or iced drink slowly
Ground yourself

Date _____   Source of Anxiety _____

Time _____   Physical Sensations _____

Place _____

Negative Beliefs

About Yourself	About Situation

What facts do you know are true?

About Yourself	About Situation

Color where you feel
sensations of anxiety

Is there a more balanced way to think about this situation

What has helped before?   What is helping now?

Coping Mechanisms

Breathe
Remind yourself that anxiety is just a feeling
Describe your surroundings in detail
Go outdoors
Sip a warm or iced drink slowly
Ground yourself

Date _____   Source of Anxiety _____

Time _____   Physical Sensations _____

Place _____

Negative Beliefs

About Yourself	About Situation

What facts do you know are true?

About Yourself	About Situation

Color where you feel
sensations of anxiety

Is there a more balanced way to think about this situation

What has helped before?   What is helping now?

Coping Mechanisms

Breathe
Remind yourself that anxiety is just a feeling
Describe your surroundings in detail
Go outdoors
Sip a warm or iced drink slowly
Ground yourself

Date _____   Source of Anxiety _____

Time _____   Physical Sensations _____

Place _____

Negative Beliefs

About Yourself	About Situation

What facts do you know are true?

About Yourself	About Situation

Color where you feel
sensations of anxiety

Is there a more balanced way to think about this situation

What has helped before?   What is helping now?

Coping Mechanisms

Breathe
Remind yourself that anxiety is just a feeling
Describe your surroundings in detail
Go outdoors
Sip a warm or iced drink slowly
Ground yourself

Date _____   Source of Anxiety _____

Time _____   Physical Sensations _____

Place _____

Negative Beliefs

About Yourself	About Situation

What facts do you know are true?

About Yourself	About Situation

Color where you feel
sensations of anxiety

Is there a more balanced way to think about this situation

What has helped before?   What is helping now?

——————————— Coping Mechanisms ———————————

Breathe
Remind yourself that anxiety is just a feeling
Describe your surroundings in detail
Go outdoors
Sip a warm or iced drink slowly
Ground yourself

Date _____   Source of Anxiety _____

Time _____   Physical Sensations _____

Place _____

Negative Beliefs

About Yourself	About Situation

What facts do you know are true?

About Yourself	About Situation

Color where you feel
sensations of anxiety

Is there a more balanced way to think about this situation

What has helped before?

What is helping now?

Coping Mechanisms

Breathe
Remind yourself that anxiety is just a feeling
Describe your surroundings in detail
Go outdoors
Sip a warm or iced drink slowly
Ground yourself

Date _____   Source of Anxiety _____

Time _____   Physical Sensations _____

Place _____

Negative Beliefs

About Yourself	About Situation

What facts do you know are true?

About Yourself	About Situation

Color where you feel
sensations of anxiety

Is there a more balanced way to think about this situation

What has helped before?

What is helping now?

Coping Mechanisms

Breathe
Remind yourself that anxiety is just a feeling
Describe your surroundings in detail
Go outdoors
Sip a warm or iced drink slowly
Ground yourself

Date _____   Source of Anxiety _____

Time _____   Physical Sensations _____

Place _____

Negative Beliefs

About Yourself	About Situation

What facts do you know are true?

About Yourself	About Situation

Color where you feel
sensations of anxiety

Is there a more balanced way to think about this situation

What has helped before?   What is helping now?

Coping Mechanisms

Breathe
Remind yourself that anxiety is just a feeling
Describe your surroundings in detail
Go outdoors
Sip a warm or iced drink slowly
Ground yourself

Date _____   Source of Anxiety _____

Time _____   Physical Sensations _____

Place _____

Negative Beliefs

About Yourself	About Situation

What facts do you know are true?

About Yourself	About Situation

Color where you feel
sensations of anxiety

Is there a more balanced way to think about this situation

What has helped before?   What is helping now?

──────── Coping Mechanisms ────────

Breathe
Remind yourself that anxiety is just a feeling
Describe your surroundings in detail
Go outdoors
Sip a warm or iced drink slowly
Ground yourself

Date _____   Source of Anxiety _____

Time _____   Physical Sensations _____

Place _____

Negative Beliefs

About Yourself	About Situation

What facts do you know are true?

About Yourself	About Situation

Color where you feel
sensations of anxiety

Is there a more balanced way to think about this situation

What has helped before?   ## What is helping now?

Coping Mechanisms

Breathe
Remind yourself that anxiety is just a feeling
Describe your surroundings in detail
Go outdoors
Sip a warm or iced drink slowly
Ground yourself

Date _____   Source of Anxiety _____

Time _____   Physical Sensations _____

Place _____

Negative Beliefs

About Yourself	About Situation

What facts do you know are true?

About Yourself	About Situation

Color where you feel
sensations of anxiety

Is there a more balanced way to think about this situation

What has helped before?   What is helping now?

———————————— Coping Mechanisms ————————————

Breathe
Remind yourself that anxiety is just a feeling
Describe your surroundings in detail
Go outdoors
Sip a warm or iced drink slowly
Ground yourself

Date _____   Source of Anxiety _____

Time _____   Physical Sensations _____

Place _____

Negative Beliefs

About Yourself	About Situation

What facts do you know are true?

About Yourself	About Situation

Color where you feel
sensations of anxiety

Is there a more balanced way to think about this situation

What has helped before?

What is helping now?

—— Coping Mechanisms ——

Breathe
Remind yourself that anxiety is just a feeling
Describe your surroundings in detail
Go outdoors
Sip a warm or iced drink slowly
Ground yourself

Date _____   Source of Anxiety _____

Time _____   Physical Sensations _____

Place _____

Negative Beliefs

About Yourself	About Situation

What facts do you know are true?

About Yourself	About Situation

Color where you feel
sensations of anxiety

Is there a more balanced way to think about this situation

What has helped before?

What is helping now?

Coping Mechanisms

Breathe
Remind yourself that anxiety is just a feeling
Describe your surroundings in detail
Go outdoors
Sip a warm or iced drink slowly
Ground yourself

Date _____   Source of Anxiety _____

Time _____   Physical Sensations _____

Place _____

Negative Beliefs

About Yourself	About Situation

What facts do you know are true?

About Yourself	About Situation

Color where you feel
sensations of anxiety

Is there a more balanced way to think about this situation

What has helped before?   What is helping now?

Coping Mechanisms

Breathe
Remind yourself that anxiety is just a feeling
Describe your surroundings in detail
Go outdoors
Sip a warm or iced drink slowly
Ground yourself

Date _____   Source of Anxiety _____

Time _____   Physical Sensations _____

Place _____

Negative Beliefs

About Yourself	About Situation

What facts do you know are true?

About Yourself	About Situation

Color where you feel
sensations of anxiety

Is there a more balanced way to think about this situation

What has helped before?   What is helping now?

Coping Mechanisms

Breathe
Remind yourself that anxiety is just a feeling
Describe your surroundings in detail
Go outdoors
Sip a warm or iced drink slowly
Ground yourself

Date _____   Source of Anxiety _____

Time _____   Physical Sensations _____

Place _____

Negative Beliefs

About Yourself	About Situation

What facts do you know are true?

About Yourself	About Situation

Color where you feel
sensations of anxiety

Is there a more balanced way to think about this situation

What has helped before?   ## What is helping now?

Coping Mechanisms
Breathe
Remind yourself that anxiety is just a feeling
Describe your surroundings in detail
Go outdoors
Sip a warm or iced drink slowly
Ground yourself

Date _____   Source of Anxiety _____

Time _____   Physical Sensations _____

Place _____

Negative Beliefs

About Yourself	About Situation

What facts do you know are true?

About Yourself	About Situation

Color where you feel
sensations of anxiety

Is there a more balanced way to think about this situation

What has helped before?   What is helping now?

———————————————— Coping Mechanisms ————————————————

Breathe
Remind yourself that anxiety is just a feeling
Describe your surroundings in detail
Go outdoors
Sip a warm or iced drink slowly
Ground yourself

Date _____   Source of Anxiety _____

Time _____   Physical Sensations _____

Place _____

Negative Beliefs

About Yourself	About Situation

What facts do you know are true?

About Yourself	About Situation

Color where you feel
sensations of anxiety

Is there a more balanced way to think about this situation

What has helped before?

What is helping now?

Coping Mechanisms

Breathe
Remind yourself that anxiety is just a feeling
Describe your surroundings in detail
Go outdoors
Sip a warm or iced drink slowly
Ground yourself

Date _____   Source of Anxiety _____

Time _____   Physical Sensations _____

Place _____

Negative Beliefs

About Yourself	About Situation

What facts do you know are true?

About Yourself	About Situation

Color where you feel
sensations of anxiety

Is there a more balanced way to think about this situation

What has helped before?

What is helping now?

Coping Mechanisms

Breathe
Remind yourself that anxiety is just a feeling
Describe your surroundings in detail
Go outdoors
Sip a warm or iced drink slowly
Ground yourself

Date _____   Source of Anxiety _____

Time _____   Physical Sensations _____

Place _____

Negative Beliefs

About Yourself	About Situation

What facts do you know are true?

About Yourself	About Situation

Color where you feel
sensations of anxiety

Is there a more balanced way to think about this situation

What has helped before?

What is helping now?

Coping Mechanisms

Breathe
Remind yourself that anxiety is just a feeling
Describe your surroundings in detail
Go outdoors
Sip a warm or iced drink slowly
Ground yourself

Date _____   Source of Anxiety _____

Time _____   Physical Sensations _____

Place _____

Negative Beliefs

About Yourself	About Situation

What facts do you know are true?

About Yourself	About Situation

Color where you feel
sensations of anxiety

Is there a more balanced way to think about this situation

What has helped before?   What is helping now?

Coping Mechanisms

Breathe
Remind yourself that anxiety is just a feeling
Describe your surroundings in detail
Go outdoors
Sip a warm or iced drink slowly
Ground yourself

Date _____   Source of Anxiety _____

Time _____   Physical Sensations _____

Place _____

Negative Beliefs

About Yourself	About Situation

What facts do you know are true?

About Yourself	About Situation

Color where you feel
sensations of anxiety

Is there a more balanced way to think about this situation

What has helped before?   What is helping now?

---- Coping Mechanisms ----

Breathe
Remind yourself that anxiety is just a feeling
Describe your surroundings in detail
Go outdoors
Sip a warm or iced drink slowly
Ground yourself

Date _____   Source of Anxiety _____

Time _____   Physical Sensations _____

Place _____

Negative Beliefs

About Yourself	About Situation

What facts do you know are true?

About Yourself	About Situation

Color where you feel
sensations of anxiety

Is there a more balanced way to think about this situation

What has helped before?   What is helping now?

Coping Mechanisms

Breathe
Remind yourself that anxiety is just a feeling
Describe your surroundings in detail
Go outdoors
Sip a warm or iced drink slowly
Ground yourself

Date _____   Source of Anxiety _____

Time _____   Physical Sensations _____

Place _____

Negative Beliefs

About Yourself	About Situation

What facts do you know are true?

About Yourself	About Situation

Color where you feel
sensations of anxiety

Is there a more balanced way to think about this situation

What has helped before?   What is helping now?

——————————— Coping Mechanisms ———————————

Breathe
Remind yourself that anxiety is just a feeling
Describe your surroundings in detail
Go outdoors
Sip a warm or iced drink slowly
Ground yourself

Date _____   Source of Anxiety _____

Time _____   Physical Sensations _____

Place _____

Negative Beliefs

About Yourself	About Situation

What facts do you know are true?

About Yourself	About Situation

Color where you feel
sensations of anxiety

Is there a more balanced way to think about this situation

What has helped before?   ## What is helping now?

Coping Mechanisms ---

Breathe
Remind yourself that anxiety is just a feeling
Describe your surroundings in detail
Go outdoors
Sip a warm or iced drink slowly
Ground yourself

Date _____   Source of Anxiety _____

Time _____   Physical Sensations _____

Place _____

Negative Beliefs

About Yourself	About Situation

What facts do you know are true?

About Yourself	About Situation

Color where you feel
sensations of anxiety

Is there a more balanced way to think about this situation

What has helped before?   What is helping now?

——————— Coping Mechanisms ———————

Breathe
Remind yourself that anxiety is just a feeling
Describe your surroundings in detail
Go outdoors
Sip a warm or iced drink slowly
Ground yourself

Date _____   Source of Anxiety _____

Time _____   Physical Sensations _____

Place _____

Negative Beliefs

About Yourself	About Situation

What facts do you know are true?

About Yourself	About Situation

Color where you feel
sensations of anxiety

Is there a more balanced way to think about this situation

What has helped before?   ## What is helping now?

Coping Mechanisms

Breathe
Remind yourself that anxiety is just a feeling
Describe your surroundings in detail
Go outdoors
Sip a warm or iced drink slowly
Ground yourself

Date _____   Source of Anxiety _____

Time _____   Physical Sensations _____

Place _____

Negative Beliefs

About Yourself	About Situation

What facts do you know are true?

About Yourself	About Situation

Color where you feel
sensations of anxiety

Is there a more balanced way to think about this situation

What has helped before?   What is helping now?

Coping Mechanisms

Breathe
Remind yourself that anxiety is just a feeling
Describe your surroundings in detail
Go outdoors
Sip a warm or iced drink slowly
Ground yourself

Date _____   Source of Anxiety _____

Time _____   Physical Sensations _____

Place _____

Negative Beliefs

About Yourself	About Situation

What facts do you know are true?

About Yourself	About Situation

Color where you feel
sensations of anxiety

Is there a more balanced way to think about this situation

What has helped before?   What is helping now?

——————————————— Coping Mechanisms ———————————————

Breathe
Remind yourself that anxiety is just a feeling
Describe your surroundings in detail
Go outdoors
Sip a warm or iced drink slowly
Ground yourself

Date _____   Source of Anxiety _____

Time _____   Physical Sensations _____

Place _____

Negative Beliefs

About Yourself	About Situation

What facts do you know are true?

About Yourself	About Situation

Color where you feel
sensations of anxiety

Is there a more balanced way to think about this situation

What has helped before?   ## What is helping now?

Coping Mechanisms

Breathe
Remind yourself that anxiety is just a feeling
Describe your surroundings in detail
Go outdoors
Sip a warm or iced drink slowly
Ground yourself

Date _____   Source of Anxiety _____

Time _____   Physical Sensations _____

Place _____

Negative Beliefs

About Yourself	About Situation

What facts do you know are true?

About Yourself	About Situation

Color where you feel
sensations of anxiety

Is there a more balanced way to think about this situation

What has helped before?   What is helping now?

Coping Mechanisms

Breathe
Remind yourself that anxiety is just a feeling
Describe your surroundings in detail
Go outdoors
Sip a warm or iced drink slowly
Ground yourself

Date _____ Source of Anxiety _____

Time _____ Physical Sensations _____

Place _____

Negative Beliefs

About Yourself	About Situation

What facts do you know are true?

About Yourself	About Situation

Color where you feel
sensations of anxiety

Is there a more balanced way to think about this situation

What has helped before?

What is helping now?

Coping Mechanisms

Breathe
Remind yourself that anxiety is just a feeling
Describe your surroundings in detail
Go outdoors
Sip a warm or iced drink slowly
Ground yourself

Date _____   Source of Anxiety _____

Time _____   Physical Sensations _____

Place _____

Negative Beliefs

About Yourself	About Situation

What facts do you know are true?

About Yourself	About Situation

Color where you feel
sensations of anxiety

Is there a more balanced way to think about this situation

What has helped before?   What is helping now?

Coping Mechanisms

Breathe
Remind yourself that anxiety is just a feeling
Describe your surroundings in detail
Go outdoors
Sip a warm or iced drink slowly
Ground yourself

Date _____   Source of Anxiety _____

Time _____   Physical Sensations _____

Place _____

Negative Beliefs

About Yourself	About Situation

What facts do you know are true?

About Yourself	About Situation

Color where you feel
sensations of anxiety

Is there a more balanced way to think about this situation

What has helped before?   What is helping now?

—————————— Coping Mechanisms ——————————

Breathe
Remind yourself that anxiety is just a feeling
Describe your surroundings in detail
Go outdoors
Sip a warm or iced drink slowly
Ground yourself

Date _____   Source of Anxiety _____

Time _____   Physical Sensations _____

Place _____

Negative Beliefs

About Yourself	About Situation

What facts do you know are true?

About Yourself	About Situation

Color where you feel
sensations of anxiety

Is there a more balanced way to think about this situation

What has helped before?   What is helping now?

––––––––––––––––– Coping Mechanisms –––––––––––––––

Breathe
Remind yourself that anxiety is just a feeling
Describe your surroundings in detail
Go outdoors
Sip a warm or iced drink slowly
Ground yourself

Date _____   Source of Anxiety _____

Time _____   Physical Sensations _____

Place _____

Negative Beliefs

About Yourself	About Situation

What facts do you know are true?

About Yourself	About Situation

Color where you feel
sensations of anxiety

Is there a more balanced way to think about this situation

What has helped before?   ## What is helping now?

Coping Mechanisms

Breathe
Remind yourself that anxiety is just a feeling
Describe your surroundings in detail
Go outdoors
Sip a warm or iced drink slowly
Ground yourself

Date _____   Source of Anxiety _____

Time _____   Physical Sensations _____

Place _____

Negative Beliefs

About Yourself	About Situation

What facts do you know are true?

About Yourself	About Situation

Color where you feel
sensations of anxiety

Is there a more balanced way to think about this situation

What has helped before?   What is helping now?

—————— Coping Mechanisms ——————

Breathe
Remind yourself that anxiety is just a feeling
Describe your surroundings in detail
Go outdoors
Sip a warm or iced drink slowly
Ground yourself

Date _____   Source of Anxiety _____

Time _____   Physical Sensations _____

Place _____

Negative Beliefs

About Yourself	About Situation

What facts do you know are true?

About Yourself	About Situation

Color where you feel
sensations of anxiety

Is there a more balanced way to think about this situation

What has helped before?   What is helping now?

────────── Coping Mechanisms ──────────

Breathe
Remind yourself that anxiety is just a feeling
Describe your surroundings in detail
Go outdoors
Sip a warm or iced drink slowly
Ground yourself

Date _____   Source of Anxiety _____

Time _____   Physical Sensations _____

Place _____

Negative Beliefs

About Yourself	About Situation

What facts do you know are true?

About Yourself	About Situation

Color where you feel
sensations of anxiety

Is there a more balanced way to think about this situation

What has helped before?

What is helping now?

Coping Mechanisms

Breathe
Remind yourself that anxiety is just a feeling
Describe your surroundings in detail
Go outdoors
Sip a warm or iced drink slowly
Ground yourself

Date _____   Source of Anxiety _____

Time _____   Physical Sensations _____

Place _____

Negative Beliefs

About Yourself	About Situation

What facts do you know are true?

About Yourself	About Situation

Color where you feel
sensations of anxiety

Is there a more balanced way to think about this situation

What has helped before?   What is helping now?

Coping Mechanisms

Breathe
Remind yourself that anxiety is just a feeling
Describe your surroundings in detail
Go outdoors
Sip a warm or iced drink slowly
Ground yourself

Date _____   Source of Anxiety _____

Time _____   Physical Sensations _____

Place _____

Negative Beliefs

About Yourself	About Situation

What facts do you know are true?

About Yourself	About Situation

Color where you feel
sensations of anxiety

Is there a more balanced way to think about this situation

What has helped before?   What is helping now?

———————————— Coping Mechanisms ————————————

Breathe
Remind yourself that anxiety is just a feeling
Describe your surroundings in detail
Go outdoors
Sip a warm or iced drink slowly
Ground yourself

Date _____   Source of Anxiety _____

Time _____   Physical Sensations _____

Place _____

Negative Beliefs

About Yourself	About Situation

What facts do you know are true?

About Yourself	About Situation

Color where you feel
sensations of anxiety

Is there a more balanced way to think about this situation

What has helped before?   What is helping now?

————— Coping Mechanisms —————

Breathe
Remind yourself that anxiety is just a feeling
Describe your surroundings in detail
Go outdoors
Sip a warm or iced drink slowly
Ground yourself

Date _____   Source of Anxiety _____

Time _____   Physical Sensations _____

Place _____

Negative Beliefs

About Yourself	About Situation

What facts do you know are true?

About Yourself	About Situation

Color where you feel
sensations of anxiety

Is there a more balanced way to think about this situation

What has helped before?   What is helping now?

──────── Coping Mechanisms ────────

Breathe
Remind yourself that anxiety is just a feeling
Describe your surroundings in detail
Go outdoors
Sip a warm or iced drink slowly
Ground yourself

Date _____   Source of Anxiety _____

Time _____   Physical Sensations _____

Place _____

Negative Beliefs

About Yourself	About Situation

What facts do you know are true?

About Yourself	About Situation

Color where you feel
sensations of anxiety

Is there a more balanced way to think about this situation

What has helped before?	What is helping now?

Coping Mechanisms

Breathe
Remind yourself that anxiety is just a feeling
Describe your surroundings in detail
Go outdoors
Sip a warm or iced drink slowly
Ground yourself

Date _____   Source of Anxiety _____

Time _____   Physical Sensations _____

Place _____

Negative Beliefs

About Yourself	About Situation

What facts do you know are true?

About Yourself	About Situation

Color where you feel
sensations of anxiety

Is there a more balanced way to think about this situation

What has helped before?

What is helping now?

——————————————— Coping Mechanisms ———————————————

Breathe
Remind yourself that anxiety is just a feeling
Describe your surroundings in detail
Go outdoors
Sip a warm or iced drink slowly
Ground yourself

Date _____   Source of Anxiety _____

Time _____   Physical Sensations _____

Place _____

Negative Beliefs

About Yourself	About Situation

What facts do you know are true?

About Yourself	About Situation

Color where you feel
sensations of anxiety

Is there a more balanced way to think about this situation

What has helped before?   What is helping now?

─────────────── Coping Mechanisms ───────────────

Breathe
Remind yourself that anxiety is just a feeling
Describe your surroundings in detail
Go outdoors
Sip a warm or iced drink slowly
Ground yourself

Date _____   Source of Anxiety _____

Time _____   Physical Sensations _____

Place _____

Negative Beliefs

About Yourself	About Situation

What facts do you know are true?

About Yourself	About Situation

Color where you feel
sensations of anxiety

Is there a more balanced way to think about this situation

What has helped before?   What is helping now?

Date _____   Source of Anxiety _____

Time _____   Physical Sensations _____

Place _____

Negative Beliefs

About Yourself	About Situation

What facts do you know are true?

About Yourself	About Situation

Color where you feel
sensations of anxiety

Is there a more balanced way to think about this situation

What has helped before?   What is helping now?

Coping Mechanisms

Breathe
Remind yourself that anxiety is just a feeling
Describe your surroundings in detail
Go outdoors
Sip a warm or iced drink slowly
Ground yourself

Date _____   Source of Anxiety _____

Time _____   Physical Sensations _____

Place _____

Negative Beliefs

About Yourself	About Situation

What facts do you know are true?

About Yourself	About Situation

Color where you feel
sensations of anxiety

Is there a more balanced way to think about this situation

What has helped before?   What is helping now?

─────────────── Coping Mechanisms ───────────────

Breathe
Remind yourself that anxiety is just a feeling
Describe your surroundings in detail
Go outdoors
Sip a warm or iced drink slowly
Ground yourself

Date _____   Source of Anxiety _____

Time _____   Physical Sensations _____

Place _____

Negative Beliefs

About Yourself	About Situation

What facts do you know are true?

About Yourself	About Situation

Color where you feel
sensations of anxiety

Is there a more balanced way to think about this situation

What has helped before?   What is helping now?

────── Coping Mechanisms ──────

Breathe
Remind yourself that anxiety is just a feeling
Describe your surroundings in detail
Go outdoors
Sip a warm or iced drink slowly
Ground yourself

Date _____   Source of Anxiety _____

Time _____   Physical Sensations _____

Place _____

Negative Beliefs

About Yourself	About Situation

What facts do you know are true?

About Yourself	About Situation

Color where you feel
sensations of anxiety

Is there a more balanced way to think about this situation

What has helped before?   ## What is helping now?

Coping Mechanisms

Breathe
Remind yourself that anxiety is just a feeling
Describe your surroundings in detail
Go outdoors
Sip a warm or iced drink slowly
Ground yourself

Date _____   Source of Anxiety _____

Time _____   Physical Sensations _____

Place _____

Negative Beliefs

About Yourself	About Situation

What facts do you know are true?

About Yourself	About Situation

Color where you feel
sensations of anxiety

Is there a more balanced way to think about this situation

What has helped before?   What is helping now?

Coping Mechanisms

Breathe
Remind yourself that anxiety is just a feeling
Describe your surroundings in detail
Go outdoors
Sip a warm or iced drink slowly
Ground yourself

Date _____   Source of Anxiety _____

Time _____   Physical Sensations _____

Place _____

Negative Beliefs

About Yourself	About Situation

What facts do you know are true?

About Yourself	About Situation

Color where you feel
sensations of anxiety

Is there a more balanced way to think about this situation

What has helped before?   What is helping now?

Coping Mechanisms

Breathe
Remind yourself that anxiety is just a feeling
Describe your surroundings in detail
Go outdoors
Sip a warm or iced drink slowly
Ground yourself

Date _____   Source of Anxiety _____

Time _____   Physical Sensations _____

Place _____

Negative Beliefs

About Yourself	About Situation

What facts do you know are true?

About Yourself	About Situation

Color where you feel
sensations of anxiety

Is there a more balanced way to think about this situation

What has helped before?   What is helping now?

Coping Mechanisms

Breathe
Remind yourself that anxiety is just a feeling
Describe your surroundings in detail
Go outdoors
Sip a warm or iced drink slowly
Ground yourself

Date _____   Source of Anxiety _____

Time _____   Physical Sensations _____

Place _____

Negative Beliefs

About Yourself	About Situation

What facts do you know are true?

About Yourself	About Situation

Color where you feel
sensations of anxiety

Is there a more balanced way to think about this situation

What has helped before?   What is helping now?

Coping Mechanisms

Breathe
Remind yourself that anxiety is just a feeling
Describe your surroundings in detail
Go outdoors
Sip a warm or iced drink slowly
Ground yourself

Date _____   Source of Anxiety _____

Time _____   Physical Sensations _____

Place _____

Negative Beliefs

About Yourself	About Situation

What facts do you know are true?

About Yourself	About Situation

Color where you feel
sensations of anxiety

Is there a more balanced way to think about this situation

What has helped before?   ## What is helping now?

Coping Mechanisms

Breathe
Remind yourself that anxiety is just a feeling
Describe your surroundings in detail
Go outdoors
Sip a warm or iced drink slowly
Ground yourself

Date _____   Source of Anxiety _____

Time _____   Physical Sensations _____

Place _____

Negative Beliefs

About Yourself	About Situation

What facts do you know are true?

About Yourself	About Situation

Color where you feel
sensations of anxiety

Is there a more balanced way to think about this situation

What has helped before?   What is helping now?

Coping Mechanisms

Breathe
Remind yourself that anxiety is just a feeling
Describe your surroundings in detail
Go outdoors
Sip a warm or iced drink slowly
Ground yourself

Date _____   Source of Anxiety _____

Time _____   Physical Sensations _____

Place _____

Negative Beliefs

About Yourself	About Situation

What facts do you know are true?

About Yourself	About Situation

Color where you feel
sensations of anxiety

Is there a more balanced way to think about this situation

What has helped before?	What is helping now?

Coping Mechanisms

Breathe
Remind yourself that anxiety is just a feeling
Describe your surroundings in detail
Go outdoors
Sip a warm or iced drink slowly
Ground yourself

Made in United States
North Haven, CT
23 May 2022

19455272R00082